PEOPLE OF NOTE

LAURENCE McKINNEY

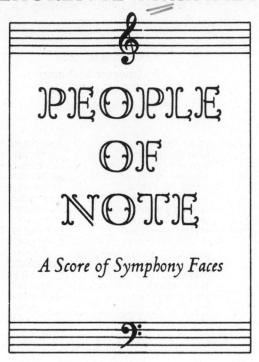

PEOPLE
OF
NOTE

A Score of Symphony Faces

PICTURES BY GLUYAS WILLIAMS

E. P. DUTTON & CO., INC.
New York, N. Y.

FIRST PRINTING ....OCTOBER, 1940
SECOND PRINTING ....OCTOBER, 1940
THIRD PRINTING ....NOVEMBER, 1940
FOURTH PRINTING ....NOVEMBER, 1940
FIFTH PRINTING ....DECEMBER, 1940
SIXTH PRINTING ....DECEMBER, 1940
SEVENTH PRINTING ....FEBRUARY, 1941
EIGHTH PRINTING ....FEBRUARY, 1941
NINTH PRINTING ....SEPTEMBER, 1941
TENTH PRINTING ....SEPTEMBER, 1941
ELEVENTH PRINTING ....OCTOBER, 1942
TWELFTH PRINTING ....NOVEMBER, 1943
THIRTEENTH PRINTING ....MARCH, 1945
FOURTEENTH PRINTING ....JANUARY, 1946
FIFTEENTH PRINTING ....SEPTEMBER, 1947
SIXTEENTH PRINTING ....APRIL, 1948
SEVENTEENTH PRINTING ....JULY, 1949

TO THE TRIO
who started this book

on its journey;

TO THE WILLIAMSES

ALICE

and

GLUYAS

and

GURNEY

•

CONTENTS

CONTENTS

PRELUDE

Time was when evenings could be spent
    In bridge, or book, or social hour,
When home musicians were content
    With vocalizing in the shower;
When theaters were used for plays
    And high school stage for graduation —
Those were the old, the quiet days
    For this unorchestrated nation.
When Peter's horn, the drum of Michael
    Were all we thought a youngster craves
Ere Wagner rode the kilocycle
    And Toscanini ruled the waves.

But music now plays such a part in
    The lives of babies, wriggling bare toes,
That even in the kindergarten
    They practice violin concertos;
And wives, of evenings, will persist
    In dragging one, a-quake with qualms,
To meet the melodies of Liszt
    And hear the harmonies of Brahms,
To watch a hundred men or so
    Equipped with catgut, wood or brass
Fiddle and bang, and wheeze and blow,
    While lazily the hours pass.

To husbands caught in such a trap
 Who wish instinctively to shout:
"Give me a book of rules, a map
 To tell me what it's all about,
To name that guy who looks so queer,
 That gaping horn which spills an earful,
Explain those pipes, back in the rear,
 And what it is that sounds so fearful."
Here is that Book and Fear Allayer,
 With which your knowledge you can shine
  up,
Here is the name of every player,
 Here is the whole symphonic line-up.

THE STRINGS

Conductor, Concert Master,* Strings
These are the most important things.

* The Concert Master is the stroke oar of the first violin section.

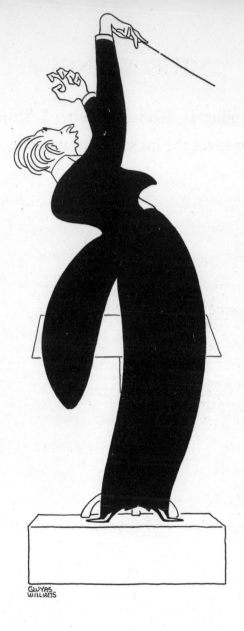

THE CONDUCTOR

This Backward Man, this View Obstructor
Is known to us as the CONDUCTOR.
He beats the time with grace and vim
And sometimes they keep up with him.
But though they're eloquent and snappy
Conductors always seem unhappy.
Their strange grimaces on the podium
Suggest bicarbonate of sodium
May be, perhaps, the proper diet
To keep their inner fires quiet.
They have to think up countless capers
To keep them in the daily papers
Which help them in financial strictures
Or fit them for the motion pictures.
Conductors worry all the while
That's why they bow, but never smile.

VIOLINS

The VIOLINS have been gregarious
Right from the time of Stradivarius
And in the worst orchestral weather
They like to string along together
Producing tones, both high and deep,
From hair of horse on gut of sheep.
And yet to play the violin
One has to take it on the chin;
But violinists take a chance
Because they know it brings romance.
With shaking head and swaying hip
Thus handily the gypsies gyp —
Thus easily the fiddlers can
Bring life and love to any man —
And so we see, from this tirade,
Why Rome burned up when Nero played.

17

VIOLA

VIOLA, there's a pretty sound
Suggesting violets, and ground
All blossoming in early spring
But, bless me, it is no such thing.
A head cold — listeners confess
Is what it sounds like more or less
And though this virtue may present
A sort of nasal armament
Violists spend the livelong day
In helping others on their way
The fiddle's friend, the cello's pal —
He helps the English Horn's morale
With envy eating out his heart
For just a tiny solo part.
No better phrase describes him than
The orchestra's forgotten man.

CELLO

When woodwinds stop, when fiddles end
That's when a CELLO needs a friend
For the composer, growing bolder,
May put things squarely on its shoulder.
Sometimes this means a real improvement —
(Beethoven's Fifth, the Second Movement)—
Or leads up to the moment when
The brasses get their wind again.
Most ladies, fluttering alone,
Prefer its mellow, manly tone
Because some cello made them cry
By playing Schumann's "Träumerei,"
And violoncellists won't reveal
The cause of this strange sex appeal.
But in the orchestra the cellos
Are treated just like regular fellows.

DOUBLE BASS

The men who have the saddest faces
Are those who play the DOUBLE BASSES
Though deep in misery their cup
They have to take it standing up,
And sawing on a clothesline string
They grunt and groan like anything.
The orchestra's last-line defense
They also see the audience
And, spying in the distant offing,
They spot the man who does the coughing —
The school girl in expectant dither —
The wife who dragged her husband with her —
The novice groping in a maze —
The critic whittling out a phrase —
And those who sleep — and those who snore
Which makes them groan and grunt
      some more.

HARP

If there's one lady in the bunch
To find her takes no special hunch
Nor sight particularly sharp
She is the girl who hugs the HARP.
The very longest tuner-upper
She has to have an early supper
And seated on a lonesome chair
Proceeds to wind up the affair.
Then she will sit and sit and wait,
Dispassionate and desolate,
Till the conductor's nod, or frown,
Sets her to stroking up and down.
And after these chromatic bits —
She simply sits and sits and sits.
A harpist must have lots of pluck —
A black silk costume — and a truck.

THE WOODWINDS

The name is quickly understood:
They're full of wind, they're made of wood *

* Except the flute which is usually metal.

FLUTE

First of the woodwinds we salute
The clever rogue who plays the FLUTE
He points his pipe the other way
Fixes his lips and starts to play.
To sound those notes — so chaste, so pure —
He blows across the embouchure
Which gives him, pardon the digression,
A strangely squirrel-like expression.
These queer highhanded players know
Another trick — the PICCOLO —
Just half as long and twice as shrill
It paralyses ears at will.
(Our artist, I deplore the fact,
Has caught him in the very act.)
The flautist's task is the pursuit
Of toot and nothing but the toot.

29

GLUYAS
WILLIAMS

OBOE

Hard to pronounce and play, the OBOE —
(With cultured folk it rhymes with
    "doughboy"
Though many an intellectual hobo
Insists that we should call it oboe)
However, be that as it may,
Whene'er the oboe sounds its A
All of the others start their tuning
And there is fiddling and bassooning.
Its plaintive note presaging gloom
Brings anguish to the concert room,
Even the player holds his breath
And scares the audience to death
For fear he may get off the key,
Which happens not infrequently.
This makes the saying understood:
"It's an ill wood wind no one blows good."

ENGLISH HORN

The ENGLISH HORN I must reveal
Has no connection with John Peel;
In fact Old John would find it meaner
To play on than a vacuum cleaner.
Its tone would make his horses skittish
For it is neither horn — nor British.
Some call it — to increase this tangle —
The Cor Anglais — or horn with angle —
Concerning which I'm glad to state
The English Horn is long and straight.
Its misery and constant dwelling
On tragedy has caused a swelling
Just where the doleful note emerges;
Imbued with melancholy surges
This makes an English Horn cadenza
Sound fearfully like influenza.

CLARINET

The happiest of the woodwinds yet
The liquid, limpid CLARINET,
Here is the instrument that's best
Wherewith to soothe the savage breast,
Invade a cobra's bailiwick,
Accompany a Hindu trick,
Or charm a tiger, stop a leopard
Or just to imitate a shepherd.
It's upper notes, uplifting, gay,
Make children dance their cares away
While others gurgled soft and deep
Give listeners a needed sleep.
And yet, should clarinetists plan
To sport like Fauns and play like Pan
And dance in amorous gyrations —
Congress would start investigations.

BASSOON

"The wedding guest here beat his breast
For he heard —" I'm sure you know the rest,
But readers constantly infer
It was the Ancient Mariner
That spoiled his day and changed his tune,
Ah, no, — "he heard the loud BASSOON."
This half a cord of wooden plumbing
Enjoys the habit of becoming
First deep and dismal, fierce and snarly,
Then laughing at you jocularly.
(A contra-bassoon can be had
Just twice as long and twice as sad.)
Italians call this bag of tricks
"Fagotto" (meaning "bunch of sticks")
Which helps to clarify the motto
I cling to: "Horn but *not* fagotto."

THE BRASSES

Even the lowest in the classes
Can guess why they call Brasses, Brasses.

TRUMPET

Remember this about the TRUMPET
You either have to like or lump it,
Some want it sweet, some want it martial
But no one ever is impartial.
In old times, at a trumpet call
A regiment would scale a wall,
But now the army, getting frugal,
Just wakes them with a blatant bugle.
To sound it tinny and acute
You stuff it with a pointed mute —
(With dance bands derby hats are normal
But symphonies are more informal.)
Some trumpeters assert it's best
To play it close against the chest
But even they are due to jump
When Angel Gabriel plays *his* trump.

FRENCH HORN

Little Boy Blue might blow his HORN
At sight of sheep or cows in corn
But that would hardly guarantee
A job in any symphony.
Should he horn in with real intent
With this left handed instrument
He'd find at once his grief would double
With bubble, bubble, coil and trouble.
He'd learn deep in the brassy throat
To poke a fist to change a note
Or try effectively to block it
While tooting toward his trouser pocket.
He'd see one ray of light, — though dim:
Conductors would be nice to him
Or find themselves impaled, forlorn,
On the dilemma of a horn.

TROMBONE

The TROMBONE causes consternation
Because it seems regurgitation
Is necessary when you play
To make the fool thing act that way.
But there's no need for one to fuss
About the guy's esophagus,
For if you closely follow it,
You'll find he doesn't swallow it.
Remember just one thought and that's:
This is the instrument that blats,
This is the instrument whose tones
May jar the marrow in your bones.
In spite of which nobody doubts
Trombonists' lives have ins and outs
Which they can make serene and full
By dint of push — and lots of pull.

GLUYAS
WILLIAMS

TUBA

Pulling its tones way up from Cuba
This mass of brass is called the TUBA
A bulky weight it seems to be
To dandle gayly on one's knee.
Though often flirting with disaster
A tuba learns to know its master
And just to show that love abounds
Emits the most outrageous sounds.
(Malignant tubas, though, for fun,
May coil about and strangle one.
So with this constantly in mind
It trains you tuba very kind.)
When Richard Wagner in a frenzy
Tried tubas in his play, "Rienzi,"
Composers thought them simply grand,
A thing I'll never understand.

PERCUSSION

These instruments appeal to boys,
They furnish all the needed noise.

TYMPANUM

The Vibrant Bowl, the TYMPANUM,
(It's also called a Kettledrum)
However lightly we may treat it,
For solid skill it's hard to beat it.
A tympanist, to make it clear
Must play it both by hand and ear,
Manipulating gadgets which
Will bring it smartly up to pitch;
Then, pots encircling him about,
He stands prepared to dish it out,
And from his tubs the flavor floats
Of tickled beats and hot rolled notes
As from these mammoth soup tureens
Come thunder storms and battle scenes.
A sweet existence we presume,
This life of everlasting boom.

51

PERCUSSION

When music gravitates to Russian
The noise you hear is called PERCUSSION
All clangorous and clattery
It's also called the Battery
Comprising gadgets — ten or more —
That clutter up a hardware store.
A fellow must be extra nimble
To beat a drum or crash a cymbal,
To bang a gong and in between
To tingle on the tambourine.
Eternal triangles, if missed
Will spoil a dainty thing by Liszt
And he must drag romantic tones
From glockenspiels and xylophones.
Far back and near the door they set him
So he escapes before they get him.

53

ENCUMBRANCES OF THE STAGE

Sometimes you'll find these added features.
Be kind: for they are all God's creatures.

THE WAGNERIAN SOPRANO

An awe-ful eyeful if you will
But here's another mouth to fill
Who may admit upon inquiry
To be an innocent Valkyrie.
Only great Wagner in "The Ring"
Could write the stuff she's built to sing
And only her pneumatic throat
Can sing the stuff that Richard wrote.
"Eva" and "Elsa," one agrees
Start but don't carry on with ease,
And it takes barrelfuls of breath
To function as "Elizabeth;"
So those who worship at their shrines
Are built on monumental lines
And while their voices rise, methinks,
The stage indubitably sinks.

GLUYAS
WILLIAMS

PIANO VIRTUOSO

From Western Coast to Eastern Seaboard
Rages the battle of the keyboard,
For storming the pianoforte
Is famous as an Indoor Sport.
Surrounded by a hundred men
Like Daniel in the Lions' Den,
The VIRTUOSO takes his seat
Preparing to resist defeat.
A few stray shots, with unconcern
He ducks, and coolly waits his turn,
It comes, and shooting flats and sharps
He knocks them for a row of harps.
Courageous as a stag at bay,
He's up, he's down, he's got away —
The fighting stops, the music ends;
They usually part as friends.

THE MIXED CHORUS

This motley mass we see before us —
This odd array — is called a CHORUS,
Or Glee Club, Choral Group or Choir,
Which Bach and Beethoven desire.
Sopranos, Altos, Tenors, Basses
Are rarely chosen for their faces
But for the strength which they employ
In shrieking out "The Hymn of Joy."
The keen-eyed listener often sees
Impending tonsillectomies
Or hears the twanging of the hordes
Of taut (and untaught) vocal cords.
One thing seems definitely certain
They should perform behind a curtain
And change the adage then to mean:
"Choruses should be heard not seen."

POSTLUDE

These are the tools and these the men
    And both together they contrive
To render Mozart young again
    And also bring you Bach alive.
In vibrant string, in tuneful bell,
    In wind through reeds, breathed on and off,
There dwells the spirit of Ravel,
    The shade of Rimsky-Korsakoff.
Go meet them, — music sets no trap —
    Advance, — between you lies no canyon,
Entice a Muse onto your lap
    You'll find she makes a grand companion;
And she'll administer a tonic
    To set your soul forever free,
So fear no harm from philharmonic
    And find the fun in symphony.